Pray,

Praise & be

Encouraged

King James Version (KJV)

P.P.E.

Vernet Clemons Nettles

VCNettles Inspirations and Letters, LLC
Montgomery, AL

https://vernetcnettles.com
www.vernetcnettles@gmail.com

Copyright - 2024

ISBN: 979-8-9913949-0-1

Printed in the United States

Table of Contents

Just A Note   4
Why P.P.E.   5

            Psalms 23   6
            The Shepherd

            Psalms 121   14
            Look Up

      Ephesians 6: 11 – 17   22
            God's Armour

         Matthew 6:9 -13   30
            Let Us Pray

         Luke 8: 43 – 48   40
      In the Midst of All Else

Benediction   43

References   44

Author's Works   45

About the Author   46

Just A Note:

The original *Pray, Praise, and be Encouraged* was published in 2020. In that edition, I used the New King James Version (NKJV) scriptural translation. Although I enjoy the language of the NKJV, there are other biblical translations that many Christians enjoy, as well. It is for this reason that a King James Version (KJV) edition of *Pray, Praise, and be Encouraged* was requested. And I am happy to oblige. *If you are one who prefers KJV – please, please, ENJOY!*

Much Love,
VCN

Why P.P.E.

Why P.P.E. - because our meditation time, our scriptures, our prayers, praise, and our worship are our protection against our struggles -our Personal Protection Equipment - our P.P.E.

Pray, Praise, & be Encouraged is written for anyone who is in need of comfort and needs to be reminded that God is ever-present and omni-present. The scripture choices are deliberately selected to remind us of a few things. First, God is our protector; He is our Shepherd. Then, we are to look up because our Help comes from above. Next, we suit up with the power of Christ and shield of faith. Finally, we acknowledge God with thanksgiving and praise. We close with a reminder that in the midst of all of what's going on, God knows us and feels us when we reach out to Him.

Thank you, Lord & Amen.

Psalm 23

"The LORD is my shepherd; I shall not want.

He maketh me to lie down in green pastures: He leadeth me beside the still waters.

He restoreth my soul: He leadeth me in the paths of righteousness for his name's sake.

Yea, though I walk through the valley of the shadow of death, I will fear no evil: for thou art with me; Thy rod and thy staff they comfort me.

Thou preparest a table before me in the presence of mine enemies: Thou anointest my head with oil; my cup runneth over.

Surely goodness and mercy shall follow me all the days of my life: And I will dwell in the house of the LORD for ever."

Psalm 23:1-6 KJV

The Shepherd

When I read the first verse of the 23rd Psalms, I begin to become calm. Whatever is troubling me begins to seem less stressful. I remember that God is my Shepherd.

When I think about a shepherd, I am reminded of someone who stands watch over the sheep, who makes sure that the sheep are fed, and who makes sure the sheep are safe. And, God is our Shepherd.

Sometimes it is hard to turn our concerns over to God. We feel as if we are out of control. But God is in control and when we allow Him to lead us, He will lead us around, through, and out of harm. Sometimes it seems as if danger will win, but every good shepherd never leaves his sheep alone and will certainly nurse them back to health.

So, the next time you are struggling or just in need of peace, lean into the fact *that the Lord is our Shepherd and we shall not want.*

Day 1

"The LORD is my shepherd; I shall not want.

Psalm 23:1 KJV

Heavenly Father, thank you for all things - for leading me and fulfilling my needs. Lord, it is my desire to follow you, to be obedient to your will, and to depend on you. Lead me, Lord, in your will; grant me your peace and safety in your bosom. In Jesus' name we pray. Amen.

Day 2

He maketh me to lie down in green pastures: He
leadeth me beside the still waters. He restoreth
my soul: He leadeth me in the paths of
righteousness for his name's sake. ."

Psalm 23:2-3 KJV

Heavenly Father, thank you for all things. My God,
thank you for your peace. Thank you for providing
me with prosperity - not just any pastures, green
pastures of life. Thank you for your restoration -
when life has tried me, you make me whole again.
Thank you, Lord for pouring your grace and mercy.
Bless your holy name. In Jesus' name we pray and
rest. Amen.

Day 3

*Yea, though I walk through the valley of the
shadow of death, I will fear no evil: for thou art
with me; Thy rod and thy staff they comfort me.*
Psalm 23:4 KJV

Heavenly Father, thank you for all things - for you
have not given us the spirit of fear. Thank you,
Lord, for being my rod AND my staff. What a
blessing to know that things may come against me,
but you are always for me. Hallelujah, Lord; Thank
you. In Jesus' name we pray. Amen.

Day 4

Thou preparest a table before me in the presence of mine enemies: Thou anointest my head with oil; my cup runneth over.

Psalm 23:5 KJV

Heavenly Father, thank you for all things - for reminding me that You are greater than my enemies. That not only will you hide me, but if it is your will, you will set me before those who strive to pull me down. Lord, I pray, bless me indeed. Keep me, Father, in your will so that I may witness the overflow you have for me. In Jesus' name we pray and seek your glory. Amen.

Day 5

Surely goodness and mercy shall follow me all the days of my life: And I will dwell in the house of the LORD for ever."

Psalm 23:6 KJV

Heavenly Father, thank you for all things - for your goodness and mercy. Lord, I know we do not deserve this, and I am grateful for your promise. When I follow you - our shepherd - you will provide for us, take care of us, and protect us from all hurt and harm. Lord, I desire to live with you forever. I desire to be in your presence. I desire to follow you. I love you, Lord, and thank you for All things. In Jesus' name we pray and praise. Amen.

"but they that wait upon the LORD shall renew their strength; they shall mount up with wings as eagles; they shall run, and not be weary; and they shall walk, and not faint."

Isaiah 40:31 KJV

Psalm 121

"I will lift up mine eyes unto the hills, From whence cometh my help.

My help cometh from the LORD, Which made heaven and earth.

He will not suffer thy foot to be moved: He that keepeth thee will not slumber.

Behold, he that keepeth Israel Shall neither slumber nor sleep.

The LORD is thy keeper: The LORD is thy shade upon thy right hand.

The sun shall not smite thee by day, Nor the moon by night.

The LORD shall preserve thee from all evil: He shall preserve thy soul.

The LORD shall preserve thy going out and thy coming in From this time forth, and even for evermore."

Psalm 121:1-8 KJV

Look Up

I love to look up into the blue sky and white clouds or the blue-black sky sprinkled with twinkling stars. Day or night, I love looking up expectantly for signs of God in the heavens.

Psalms 23 tell us that the Lord is our Shepherd. And, Psalms 121 tells us that the Lord is our help and our keeper. The Psalmist, David, declares that God will not allow us to stumble. He keeps us both night and day, and He will preserve our very soul. David reminds us that God watches over us.

When I read this Psalm, I am reminded that we do not have to struggle alone. God promises to keep us from stumbling, to shade us in times of storm, and to preserve us from evil, always.

So, when I look up to the heavens, each day or two or three times a day, I am looking expectantly because God has promised His very present care, from this time forth, and even forevermore.

Day 6

"I will lift up mine eyes unto the hills, From whence cometh my help. My help cometh from the LORD, Which made heaven and earth.

Psalm 121:1-2 KJV

Heavenly Father, thank you for all things. Father, thank you for reminding us that you are my help. You are the author of all things. Father, thank you for comfort – the comfort of knowing that you are present as I lift our eyes towards heaven. In Jesus' name we pray. Amen.

Day 7

"He will not suffer thy foot to be moved: He that keepeth thee will not slumber."

Psalm 121:3 KJV

My Lord, My Father, thank you for all things, for your certainty. Thank you for reminding us that when I depend on you, you will give me a firm foundation and you will not allow me to stumble. And, thank you for keeping me through all things and at all times. In Jesus' name we pray and praise. Amen.

Day 8

"He will not suffer thy foot to be moved: He that keepeth thee will not slumber. Behold, he that keepeth Israel Shall neither slumber nor sleep."

Psalm 121:3-4 KJV

Heavenly Father, thank you Lord. Thank you for assuring me that as you care and keep a nation, you can care and keep me. Glory Hallelujah. Lord, thank you for reminding me that in the midst of everybody else and everything else going on in this world, you see me – you know me. In Jesus' name we pray and shout Glory. Amen.

Day 9

*"The LORD is thy keeper: The LORD is thy shade
upon thy right hand. The sun shall not smite thee
by day, Nor the moon by night."*

Psalm 121:5-6 KJV

Heavenly Father, thank you for all things. Father,
thank you for keeping me, for shielding me from
things seen (by day) and not seen (by night).
Thank you for being my keeper and my care.
Father, we need you and we depend on you. In
Jesus' name we pray and praise your name. Amen.

Day 10

"The LORD shall preserve thee from all evil: He shall preserve thy soul. The LORD shall preserve thy going out and thy coming in From this time forth, and even for evermore."

Psalm 121:7-8 KJV

Glory, Glory, Hallelujah, Lord! Thank you for preserving me from evil, for being my keeper from this moment forward, for now and for always. Father, I give my life to you. Thank you for being the protector of my soul. Father, I give myself to you. In Jesus' name we pray and praise. Amen.

""Have not I commanded thee? Be strong and of a
good courage; be not afraid, neither be thou
dismayed: for the LORD thy God is with thee
whithersoever thou goest."

Joshua 1:9 KJV

Ephesians 6

"Put on the whole armour of God, that ye may be able to stand against the wiles of the devil.

For we wrestle not against flesh and blood, but against principalities, against powers, against the rulers of the darkness of this world, against spiritual wickedness in high places.

Wherefore take unto you the whole armour of God, that ye may be able to withstand in the evil day, and having done all, to stand.

Stand therefore, having your loins girt about with truth, and having on the breastplate of righteousness;

and your feet shod with the preparation of the gospel of peace;

above all, taking the shield of faith, wherewith ye shall be able to quench all the fiery darts of the wicked.

And take the helmet of salvation, and the sword of the Spirit, which is the word of God:"

Ephesians 6:11-17 KJV

God's Armour

Every now and again, life places us in a situation where we have to make a stand for or against something or somebody. A lot of times, we end of standing by ourselves. But we are never alone when we depend on God.

"The armour of God that surrounds us is in His Love. We put on Truth, Honesty, Peace, Faith, Salvation, and the Holy Spirit. When we add these skills to our daily lives; when we allow these behaviors to become a part of who we are; when we invite the Holy Spirit into our daily presence, we are able to stand firm as life challenges us.

Being wrapped in God's armour does not mean challenges and trouble won't come. Being wrapped in God's armour means we have a defense; we have someone powerful in our corner. We have the Love who allows us to be strong and courageous in Christ."

(Nettles, Moments of Grace, 2019)

Day 11

""Put on the whole armour of God, that ye may be able to stand against the wiles of the devil. For we wrestle not against flesh and blood, but against principalities, against powers, against the rulers of the darkness of this world, against spiritual wickedness in high places."

Ephesians 6:11-12 KJV

Heavenly Father, thank you for all things - for reminding me to be aware and steadfast. Remind me, Lord, to be mindful of power and wickedness used to influence me to change my mind, to change my heart, or to lose track of your purpose for me. Strengthen my heart so that through your Word and your Love, I stand firm. In Jesus' name we pray and praise. Amen.

(Nettles, Moments of Grace, 2019)

Day 12

"Stand therefore, having your loins girt about with truth, and having on the breastplate of righteousness;"

Ephesians 6:14 KJV

Heavenly Father, thank you for all things - for your covering. Thank you for reminding me that truth and integrity matters; that my heart's righteousness is my shield. Thank you for reminding me that my strength and courage comes when I lead with these attributes - truth and a loving heart. In Jesus' name we pray. Amen.

(Nettles, Moments of Grace, 2019)

Day 13

**"and your feet shod with the preparation of the
gospel of peace;"**

Ephesians 6:15 KJV

Heavenly Father, thank you for all things - for
peace. Thank you for a peace in my heart that
surpasses understanding. Thank you for a peace in
my mouth that causes me to speak peace into my
life and my situation, even though I may not always
understand. And, thank you for the shoes of peace,
so that as I walk through my day, others see peace
moving and seek it also. Father, thank you for
these blessings that I have now and seek for each
tomorrow. In Jesus' name we pray and praise you
in advance. Amen.

(Nettles, Moments of Grace, 2019)

Day 14

"above all, taking the shield of faith, wherewith ye shall be able to quench all the fiery darts of the wicked."

Ephesians 6:16 KJV

Heavenly Father, thank you for all things - for the fire extinguisher that is faith. Thank you for reminding me that fiery darts will come, but when I operate in faith, my fear, unrest, disappointment, challenges, my _____ will not defeat me. Thank you, Lord, for reminding me that my faith is my constant connection to you, your Love, and your covering. Thank you, Lord, for ALL things. In Jesus' name we pray and praise God. Amen.

(Nettles, Moments of Grace, 2019)

Day 15

"And take the helmet of salvation, and the sword of the Spirit, which is the word of God;"

Ephesians 6:17 KJV

Heavenly Father, thank you for all things. Father, thank you for my helmet - my covering. Cover my mind and protect my thoughts against the influence of the enemy. Remind me, Father, to filter out the negative, the accusations, the doubt, my _____, and focus on the joy and hope that you have given me. And, thank you for the sword of the Holy Spirit - for reminding me that this battle is not mine it is Yours, and your Spirit is an ever-present protection. Glory Hallelujah!!!! Thank you, Father, for your armour of protection. In Jesus' name we pray, praise, and Hallelujah dance. Amen.

(Nettles, Moments of Grace, 2019)

""But thou, when thou prayest, enter into thy closet, and when thou hast shut thy door, pray to thy Father which is in secret; and thy Father which seeth in secret shall reward thee openly."

Matthew 6:6 KJV

Matthew 6: 9 – 13
The Lord's Prayer

"After this manner therefore pray ye: Our Father which art in heaven, Hallowed be thy name.

Thy kingdom come. Thy will be done in earth, as it is in heaven.

Give us this day our daily bread.

And forgive us our debts, as we forgive our debtors.

And lead us not into temptation, but deliver us from evil: For thine is the kingdom, and the power, and the glory, for ever. Amen."

Matthew 6:9-13 KJV

Let us Pray

As children we are taught *The Lord's Prayer*. We learned to say it every night and we repeated it proudly. But did we always know what the words meant? I was so thankful when I began to understand all the words I had so lovingly repeated for years.

This prayer says all the things we want to say to God. *"Hello Father, we adore you. We want your will for our lives. We thank you for your daily portion. Please forgive us for our sins, as we forgive others. Help us to avoid the temptations of our lives; and deliver us from danger. You are God, all powerful. We love you. We adore you. Amen.*

As I relearned my prayer, I realized that as we ask God to forgive us, we must also forgive others. I also learned to focus on asking for His will for my life. God is always listening for our honest communication with him. As we grow in Christ, let us continue to seek him through praise, worship, and thanksgiving in prayer.

Day 16

*""After this manner therefore pray ye: Our
Father which art in heaven, Hallowed be thy
name."*

Matthew 6:9 KJV

Heavenly Father, thank you for all things - for
your Word that speaks to us daily. Father, thank
you for reminding us to keep your name holy, to
keep your name in reverence. Thank you for
reminding us that we are a part of you, that our
lives represent you - and is a reflection of your
name. Thank you, Father, for reminding us that it
is not just the words we say but how we behave
that honors you. Guide us, we pray, in Jesus' name.
Amen.

(Nettles, www.vcndailypray.com, August 16, 2017)

Day 17

"Thy kingdom come. Thy will be done in earth, as it is in heaven."

Matthew 6:10 KJV

Heavenly Father, thank you for all things - for your will and purpose for my life. Forgive us, Father, when we do what "we" think - when we arrange our lives for what we want. Help us, Father, to yield to you, to seek your path, to glorify you. Remind us, that your plans are for our good. We seek your will in our lives. Guide us, we pray, in Jesus' name. Amen.

(Nettles, www.vcndailypray.com, August 17, 2017)

Day 18

"Give us this day our daily bread."

Matthew 6:11 KJV

Heavenly Father, thank you for all things - for giving us our daily portion. Father, help us to remember during our trials that you are always a provider, always a sustainer. We are always clear when things are well and we worry when there are challenges. But the proof is all around us, when we focus on you. Thank you, Lord, for your promises. In Jesus' name we pray and praise. Amen.

(Nettles, www.vcndailypray.com, August 18, 2017)

Day 19

"And forgive us our debts, as we forgive our debtors."

Matthew 6:12 KJV

"and forgive us our sins, as we have forgiven those who sin against us."

Matthew 6:12 NLT

Heavenly Father, thank you for all things – for conviction. Thank you for reminding us that you are the ultimate example. We ask always for your forgiveness, help us, Lord, to forgive others as you have forgiven us. Help us to be gracious towards others and to love unconditionally – to love as you love us. In Jesus' name we reflect and pray. Amen.

Day 20

"And lead us not into temptation, but deliver us from evil:"

Matthew 6:13a KJV

Heavenly Father, thank you for all things - for your guidance in all things. Keep us from slipping into temptations seen and unseen, the dangers of our fears, and pride of our choices - the choices that seem small but build into larger missteps. Help us, Lord, to set our sights on you so that all of our choices align with your love and your will. You have made us for victory; keep us in your grace; deliver us into your presence. For these and many other blessings of your grace and mercy we pray. Amen.

(Nettles, www.vcndailypray.com, November 20, 2015)

"For thine is the kingdom, and the power, and the glory, for ever. Amen."

Matthew 6:13b KJV

Day 21

A Devotional of Faith

Luke 8

"And a woman having an issue of blood twelve years, which had spent all her living upon physicians, neither could be healed of any,

came behind him, and touched the border of his garment: and immediately her issue of blood stanched.

And Jesus said, Who touched me? When all denied, Peter and they that were with him said, Master, the multitude throng thee and press thee, and sayest thou, Who touched me?

And Jesus said, Somebody hath touched me: for I perceive that virtue is gone out of me.

And when the woman saw that she was not hid, she came trembling, and falling down before him, she declared unto him before all the people for what cause she had touched him, and how she was healed immediately.

And he said unto her, Daughter, be of good comfort: thy faith hath made thee whole; go in peace."

Luke 8:43-48 KJV

In the Midst of All Else

"How often do we feel that with so very much going on around us, that maybe our issues are not so important? We get lost in the crowd of everybody else and their stuff. It feels like what somebody else needs is more important than what we need."

In this chapter of Luke, the woman with the issue of blood deliberately and purposefully reaches out to touch Jesus. She desperately wants to be healed. Although hiding in the crowd, she touched Him and he noticed. One purposeful and deliberate act, and she was healed!

"Praise to Our Father, who finds our very presence in His life to be significant. He knew of her existence. God knows each of us and can find us and comfort us in the midst of all else. Hallelujah!"

Prayer:

Father God, we thank you for your omniscient and omnipotent awesomeness. Thank you for knowing the hurts of our hearts and for possessing the power to heal them. We praise you for knowing our needs and for being a God of proximity that we may reach you. Thank you for never being too busy and always attentive to our needs. In Jesus' most precious name we pray. Amen.

(Nettles, Why Should I Be Bound, 2018)

Benediction

"Now unto him that is able to do exceeding abundantly above all that we ask or think, according to the power that worketh in us, unto him be glory in the church by Christ Jesus throughout all ages, world without end. Amen."

Ephesians 3:20-21 KJV

References

Nettles, V.C. (2018). Day 23 – In the Midst of All Else. *Why Should I Be Bound? Musing on a Journey with God* (pp. 115 – 117) Maitland: Xulon Press.

Nettles, V.C. (2019) Moments of Grace – A 2020 Devotional Planner (pp. 106, 108, 110, 112, 114) Jeffersonville: BK Royston Publishing.

https://www.vcndailypray.com/
(Several prayers have originally posted on my daily prayer website – Another Day's Journey.)

http://www.youversion.com/

Recent Author's Works

Beautiful, Just Like Me (2022)

Smart, Just Like Me (2023)

Moments of Grace: A New Beginning (2023)

Walking With Gace: A Fresh Start (2023)

Sufficient Grace: New Mercies Each Day (2023)

Prayers for the Journey (2023)

Dear God, Is My Mommy with You? (2024)

Dear God, Is My Daddy with You? (2024)

To see more titles and purchase, visit:
www.vernetcnettles.com
www.amazon.com

About the Author

Vernet Clemons Nettles, EdD is a parent, educator, poet, and writing coach. Currently, she resides in Montgomery, AL. Throughout the years, she has served in various capacities of church service and has retired from the public school system.

She shares her daily prayers on her website: Another Day's Journey - www.vcndailypray.com.

To connect with Vernet C. Nettles, visit www.vernetcnettles.com

Made in the USA
Columbia, SC
23 September 2024

42150635R00026